Alaska Fish Species

Game Fish & Panfish

Billy Grinslott & Kinsey Marie Books

ISBN - 9781965098851

Trout perch are silvery or nearly transparent with dark spots along their sides. Trout perch are small, typically reaching a total length of 3 to 5 inches with some individuals growing up to 8 inches. They inhabit lakes and rivers, usually over sand or gravel bottoms. Trout-perch are nocturnal feeders, they feed at night, consuming aquatic insects and small crustaceans.

Pond smelts are small, silvery fish, commonly found in freshwater lakes, rivers, and ponds, and are anadromous, meaning they spend part of their lives in freshwater and part in saltwater. Pond smelt are known for being small, with most individuals rarely exceeding 8 inches in length. The common length of pond smelt is around 4.4 inches. In some regions, smelts are celebrated through festivals, such as the Smelt Fry.

Pacific herring are known for their schooling behavior, forming large groups that can extend for several kilometers. Pacific herring feed on tiny organisms like phytoplankton and zooplankton. Pacific herring typically grow to a length of around 18 inches and weigh up to 1.2 pounds. While they can grow to 18 inches, a typical adult size is closer to 13 inches.

Shiner perch are common in bays, estuaries, and coastal streams along the Pacific coast, ranging from California to Alaska. They prefer shallow waters, often found near eelgrass beds, pilings of wharves and piers, and in backwaters. They have a silvery body and can be distinguished by their oval-shaped body. Shiner perch have the ability to live in both salty ocean water and the fresher water in coastal wetlands.

Cisco fish, also known as lake herring, are cold-water fish, part of the trout and salmon family, that thrive in lakes and rivers, often forming large schools. Cisco is silvery with faint pink to purple iridescence on their sides. Cisco are also commonly called tullibee or lake herring. While they can reach a length of over 18 inches, they are generally smaller. The largest recorded cisco fish caught in Alaska, also known as a Bering cisco, measured at 22 inches long and weighed approximately 5 pounds.

The Alaska blackfish is known for its ability to breathe air and thrive in cold, oxygen deficient waters, making it the only air-breathing fish in the Arctic. They inhabit low-lying lakes, bogs, and rivers with dense vegetation in Alaska. In winter, when dissolved oxygen levels drop under the ice, they gather near openings in the ice to gulp air and stay active. They are small fish, typically reaching about 8 inches in length.

Mottled sculpins are small, bottom-dwelling fish with a flattened body shape, large pectoral fins, and a unique camouflage pattern, often found in clear, fast-flowing waters with rocky substrates, and they are known for their ambush hunting tactics. Sculpins have very large mouths and can swallow items nearly as large as themselves.

The burbot, also known as the eel pout. They get their name because they have a serpent-like or eel-like body. They can wrap their tail around things. There's nothing to worry about if you catch one, they may try to wrap their tail around your arm, but they are harmless. Burbots are adapted to cold water and are found in large, cold rivers, lakes, and reservoirs, primarily preferring freshwater habitats. Burbots are also known as eelpout, lingcod, and lawyer. The largest burbot caught in Alaska, and the state record, weighed 24 pounds, 12 ounces.

Black cod are also known as sablefish. Black cod thrives in the cold, deep waters of the Pacific Ocean, often found at depths of over 3,000 feet. They are dark gray to black on their upper body with a lighter gray underside. Black cod are long-lived, with some individuals reaching over 90 years of age. The largest black cod, or sablefish, caught in Alaska has been recorded at a length of 45 inches and a weight of 55 pounds.

Lingcod is a bottom-dwelling fish found along the North American Pacific Coast, are known for their large size. They can grow up to 5 feet long and weigh over 80 pounds. Lingcod are solitary fish and usually stray only a short distance from their rocky home base at the bottom. Lingcod have a large head and mouth, and 18 large, sharp teeth, earning them the nickname buckethead. The largest lingcod caught in Alaska weighed 82.6 pounds and was 55 inches long,

Sturgeons have sharp spines on their back, so be careful when handling them. Sturgeon skin is made of bony plates called scutes, which can be sharp on young fish. Sturgeons have been around since the dinosaur days. Sturgeons mostly live in large, freshwater lakes and rivers. Their average lifespan is 50 to 60 years. White sturgeon are the largest fish in North America, and lake sturgeon can weigh over 800 pounds. Caviar is made from the eggs of sturgeon. The heaviest documented white sturgeon weighed 1,386 pounds.

Longnose sucker fishes are part of the sucker family and are known for their bottom-facing mouths and fleshy lips which they use to suck food off the bottom. Their lips extend outward, and they use suction like a vacuum cleaner to suck up algae off the bottom. They are native to the northern parts of North America and live in cold, clear waters of local rivers and streams. Longnose suckers in Alaska are usually shorter than 23 inches.

Whitefish are related to salmon and trout. They are known for their deep-bodied, silvery appearance and are a major part of the lake's ecosystem. They typically grow to 17-22 inches and range from 1.5-4 pounds. Whitefish are a popular and valuable commercial fish, generating income for commercial fisheries. Whitefish are also known as, whiting, and shad. The largest record sport-caught sheefish (a type of whitefish) in Alaska weighed 53 pounds.

Sablefish inhabit the deep, cold waters of the North Pacific, often found on the continental slope at depths of 650 to 9,800 feet. Adult sablefish can grow to lengths of up to 45 inches and weights of up to 55 pounds, especially in Alaskan waters. Sablefish are opportunistic feeders, consuming a variety of fish, squid, euphausiids, and jellyfish. Sablefish are the target of a sustainably managed commercial and recreational fishery in the Pacific Northwest.

Rockfish are cool because they come in many colors. Some of them are the Yelloweye, Vermillion, Copper, Black, Blue and Canary rockfish Their name comes from their habit of hiding among rocks, They can remain motionless for long periods of time, staying in one place. Rockfish are one of the longest-living fishes, possibly living to 200 years old.

Pacific Ocean perch are a type of rockfish. They grow slowly, reaching about 20 inches long and weighing around 4 pounds. They can live for up to 98 years. They have a variety of colors, mostly red and oranges, and many can have color blotches. Pacific Ocean Perches are found off the Pacific coast of North America from California to Alaska and are a good source of protein and nutrients. They are also known as redfish, red bream, or Pacific rockfish.

Prowfish have an elongated, laterally compressed body, a short, blunt snout, and a large mouth with small, sharp teeth in a single row. They spend most of their time on or near the bottom in rocky areas. Prowfish come in a variety of different colors. Typically, they are bluish grey to olive brown with small dark spots, grading to lighter shades. Prowfish in Alaska can grow up to about 35 inches long.

Atka mackerel prefer habitats with strong currents. Atka mackerel have vertical bands on their bodies, which are normally yellowish to brown in color. Atka mackerel are found in the Aleutian Islands, the Komandorskiye Islands, and the Gulf of Alaska. Atka mackerel can live up to 14 years. The largest Atka mackerel recorded in Alaska was 22.2 inches long and weighed 4.4 pounds.

Pollock grow quickly and have a relatively short lifespan of about 12 years. They are found in large schools in waters between 330 and 985 feet deep but can be found as deep as 3,300 feet. Pollock make daily vertical migrations to forage, moving deeper in the water column at night and shallower during the day. Pollock is also known as the coalfish. Alaska pollock, a member of the cod family, can grow as long as 3 feet, but are typically 12 to 20 inches in length and weigh 1 to 3 pounds.

Walleye pollock are also known as Alaska pollock. They can grow up to 3 feet in length and live up to 22 years. They migrate seasonally between spawning and feeding areas. They have a delicate, sweet flavor and many people love to eat them. Pollock fillets become the fish sticks and fish fillets familiar to many people who eat fish. They are found in the North Pacific Ocean and the Bearing Sea.

Cod are a popular food fish in the North. They inhabit cold waters of the Atlantic and Pacific. They are bottom-dwelling, schooling fish that can grow up to 6 feet long and live for up to 20 years. They have a barbel, a whisker-like sensory organ on their chin, which helps them find food. They can change color, varying from grey green to reddish-brown. A group of cod is called a lap. The largest cod fish caught in Alaska, a lingcod, weighed 85 pounds and was 60 inches long.

The Northern Pike is one of the most sought-after fish for anglers. It got its name because it likes to live in cooler water mainly in the northern states of North America. The northern pike is a very aggressive predator. They don't like to live in groups with other fish, they are very territorial and like to live alone. Their behavior is closely affected by weather conditions. Northern pike have eyes that can move in almost any direction. Northern pike can remain still for long periods of time. The largest sport-caught northern pike in Alaska weighed 38 pounds, 8 ounces.

Steelhead trout are anadromous, meaning they are born in freshwater, migrate to the ocean for their adult lives, and then return to freshwater to reproduce. Steelhead trout can grow to lengths of up to 45 inches and weights of up to 55 pounds. Steelhead trout are generally slenderer and more streamlined, which helps them navigate ocean currents and strong river currents. The largest steelhead trout caught in Alaska weighed 42 pounds and 3 ounces.

The rainbow trout gets its name because of its brilliant colors. Rainbow trout populations are good indicators of water pollution because they can only survive in clean waters. They like to live in rivers and streams. Rainbow trout rank among the top five most sought game fish in North America. Rainbow trout are also known as redband trout and steelhead trout. Rainbow trout have been commercially farmed since 1870.

The cutthroat's name comes from the bright red or orange slash-like markings under their jaws. There are several subspecies of cutthroat trout, including the coastal, Yellowstone, and Lahontan cutthroat. They inhabit a variety of cold, freshwater environments, including small streams, rivers, and lakes. Mature cutthroat trout can range from 6 to 40 inches in length. The largest cutthroat trout caught in Alaska weighed 8 pounds, 6 ounces.

Despite their name, Dolly Varden trout are actually a type of char. There are two forms of Dolly Varden trout in Alaska, a northern form and a southern form. The name Dolly Varden is derived from a character in Charles Dickens novel Barnaby Rudge, known for her bright, colorful clothing. Dolly Varden is the most widely distributed salmonid in Alaska. Dolly Varden can grow to a significant size, with the current Alaska record being 27.7 pounds, the Length was 41 ½ inches.

Chinook salmon are hatch in freshwater streams and rivers then migrate out to the saltwater environment of the ocean to feed and grow. Chinook salmon are the largest of the Pacific Ocean salmon, that's how they got the name king salmon. Chinook salmon are also known as King Salmon and when they reach over 30 pounds, some people refer to them as Tyee. The largest Chinook salmon caught in Alaska weighed 126 pounds and was caught in a fish trap. The world sport fishing record is a 97-pound 4-ounce fish caught in the Kenai River in 1985.

Coho salmon, also known as silver salmon, live in both fresh and saltwater, migrating from the ocean to freshwater streams to spawn. They are known for their silver-colored bodies and red sides during spawning. During spawning, males develop a strongly hooked snout and large teeth. Adult coho salmon typically weigh 8 to 12 pounds and are 24 to 30 inches long. The largest Coho salmon, also known as Silver Salmon, caught in Alaska weighed 26 pounds 11 ounces.

Chum salmon, also known as dog salmon, are a common Pacific salmon species. They are the most widely distributed of all Pacific salmon species, found in coastal streams from Arctic Alaska to San Diego, California. Chum salmon have a dark olive-green back and dark maroon sides, with irregular greenish vertical bars on the sides, and no spots on the back or tail. Chum salmon are medium-sized fish, averaging 24 inches in length and between 9.7 to 22 lbs in weight. The largest chum salmon caught in Alaska weighed 35 pounds, was 38.5 inches long.

Sockeye salmon, known for their vibrant red skin, are fish that hatch in freshwater, migrate to the ocean, and then return to freshwater spawn. After spending 2-3 years in the ocean, sockeye salmon return to their natal streams to spawn. They range in size from 24 to 33 inches in length and weigh between 5 and 15 pounds. The largest sockeye salmon caught in Alaska, and the world record, weighed 16 pounds and was 31 inches long.

Pink salmon have the shortest lifespan of any Pacific salmon species, living only two years. The pink color of their skin comes from the crustaceans they eat, which are rich in a reddish-orange pigment. Pink salmon are one of the most abundant species of Pacific salmon. Pink salmon hatch in freshwater streams and migrate to the ocean after a few months. The largest pink salmon caught in Alaska weighed 13 pounds, 10.6 ounces, was 32 inches long.

Flounder are born with an eye on each side of their head, but as they develop, one eye migrates to the other side, resulting in both eyes being on the same side of the body, facing upwards. Flounders can change the color and pattern of their skin to match the seafloor, helping them blend in. Flounders spend most of their time on the seafloor. The largest starry flounder caught in Alaska, taken with a spear gun, weighed 13.2 pounds.

The Halibut is a weird fish. They start out swimming upright like most other fish, with an eye on each side. As they grow, one of their eyes moves to the other side and then they invert and swim on their side. The flounder and the Halibut are a couple of fish that swim sideways. They are also known as flat fish. Halibut can grow to be over 8 feet long and 5 feet wide. They live on the bottom of the ocean, typically. The largest Halibut in Alaska was 515 pounds.

The Arctic char is part of the salmon family. It is highly adapted to cold frigid waters. Arctic chars live farther north than any other freshwater fish. It can be found in lakes only 500 miles from the North pole. No other fish lives anywhere farther north than the Arctic Char. Arctic char are an important food source for northern communities. Arctic chars are similar in shape to salmon and trout, but vary in color depending on the time of year and location. The largest Arctic char caught in Alaska, and the current state record, weighed over 19 pounds.

The Arctic grayling is one of the most beautiful freshwater fishes. Its most striking physical feature is the large, sail like dorsal or backfin. The Arctic grayling comes in a wide array of colors. Their color can vary from stream to stream. The sides of the body, fins and head can be freckled with spots. They can grow to be 30 inches long and weigh up to 8.4 pounds. They can travel more than 100 miles in one year. The largest recorded Arctic grayling caught in Alaska measured 24 inches long and weighed 5 pounds, 1 ounce.

The lake trout is one of the biggest of the trout family. The biggest lake trout caught was 72 pounds. Lake trout like to live in lakes that are deep. They like being in the cool water in the deep parts of a lake. They have been reported to live up to 70 years in some Canadian lakes. The largest lake trout caught in Alaska weighed 47 pounds.

Fun Facts About Alaska Fish

1 - Chinook Salmon, King Salmon, are Alaska's state fish, known for their large size.

2 - The longest known trip ever taken by a salmon, was a Chinook salmon that traveled 2389 miles upstream to spawn.

3 - Alaska Blackfish can breathe both in the water and out.

4 - Salmon swim upstream and jump nearly ten feet in the air to get past waterfalls.

5 - Alaska salmon start out in freshwater before migrating to the ocean where they adapt to seawater.

6 - The striking color of sockeye salmon flesh comes from eating plankton and krill while in the ocean.

7 - Landlocked sockeye salmon rarely grow to more than 14 inches in length and are called kokanee.

8 - The biggest fish caught in Alaska was a Pacific halibut weighing 459 pounds.

Author Page

Thanks

www.ingramcontent.com/pod-product-compliance
Lightning Source LLC
Chambersburg PA
CBHW060853270326
41934CB00002B/116